NATIONAL GEOGRAPHIC | **GLOBAL ISSUES**

M000106078

POLLUTION

Andrew J. Milson, Ph.D.
Content Consultant
University of Texas at Arlington

Acknowledgments

Grateful acknowledgment is given to the authors, artists, photographers, museums, publishers, and agents for permission to reprint copyrighted material. Every effort has been made to secure the appropriate permission. If any omissions have been made or if corrections are required, please contact the Publisher.

Instructional Consultant: Christopher Johnson, Evanston, Illinois

Teacher Reviewer: Mary Trichel, Atascocita Middle School, Humble, Texas

Photographic Credits

Front Cover, Inside Front Cover, Title Page ©Joel Sartore/National Geographic Stock. **4** (bg) ©AP Photo/Oded Balilty. **6** (bg) ©Pantelis Saitas/epa/Corbis. **8** (bg) Mapping Specialists. **10** (bg) ©Adam Jones/Visuals Unlimited/Corbis. **12** (cr) ©Dan Lamont/Corbis. (t) ©Peter Essick/Aurora Photos. **14** (bg) ©Peter Essick/National Geographic Stock. **16** (bg) ©Antoine Gyori/Sygma/Corbis. **17** (bl) ©Nikolai Ignatiev/Alamy. **18** (tr) ©Science Faction/SuperStock. **19** (bg) ©REUTERS/Denis Sinyakov. **20** (bg) ©REUTERS/Denis Sinyakov. **22** (bg) ©Universal Images Group/SuperStock. **23** (bl) ©AP Photo/Rick Rycroft. **24** (t) ©REUTERS/Daniel Munoz. **27** (t) ©Bob Daemmrich/Corbis. **28** (tr) ©Urban Zone/Alamy. **30** (tr) ©akg-images/RIA Nowosti. (br) ©James P. Blair/National Geographic Stock. **31** (bg) ©Axiom Photographic Limited/SuperStock. (tr) ©Universal Images Group/SuperStock. (br) ©Diego Giudice/Archivolatino/Redux. (bl) ©Pantelis Saitas/epa/Corbis.

For permission to use material from this text or product, submit all requests online at www.cengage.com/permissions

Further permissions questions can be emailed to permissionrequest@cengage.com

Visit National Geographic Learning online at www.NGSP.com.

Visit our corporate website at www.cengage.com.

Printed in the USA.

RR Donnelley, Jefferson City, MO

ISBN: 978-07362-97851

12 13 14 15 16 17 18 19 20 21

10 9 8 7 6 5 4 3 2 1

Polluted PLAN

HOW IS POLLUTION THREATENING OUR HEALTH AND OUR PLANET?

Dirty air, miles of waste, and water that's not safe to drink—welcome to our polluted planet! **Pollution** is caused by **contaminants**, substances that poison our environment. Used chemicals, discarded household goods, exhaust fumes, plastics, industrial materials, and animal waste are turning land and the oceans into garbage dumps. The pollution is a result of the demands we as consumers create for products that contribute to harming our environment. Unchecked, pollution has the potential to ruin our health and our planet.

Cyclists cross a smog-filled Tiananmen Square in Beijing, China.

AIR THAT IS HARD TO BREATHE

Recently the World Health Organization reported that 3.3 million people died in a calendar year from the effects of air pollution. That's almost a hundred times more than those dying in automobile accidents in the United States! About half of these deaths were caused by air pollution from auto emissions. Today air pollution threatens billions of people, especially in urban areas.

Polluted air contains a mix of contaminants including both gases and tiny bits of matter. Among the most common gases are **carbon dioxide** (CO_2) and ozone. Carbon dioxide slows reflexes while ozone reduces lung capacity. Another gas, nitrogen dioxide, strengthens the symptoms of allergies and asthma. Tiny bits of matter called **particulates**, such as dust and soot, contribute to heart and lung diseases.

This landfill in Athens, Greece, receives 3,500 tons of waste every day.

THE WORLD'S MOST TOXIC POLLUTION PROBLEMS, 2011		
PROBLEM	POLLUTANT	ESTIMATED POPULATION AT RISK
Small-scale mining	Mercury	3.5 million
Industrial parks	Lead	3.0 million
Agricultural production	Pesticides	2.2 million
Lead smelting	Lead	2.0 million
Tannery (leather) operations	Chromium	1.8 million

Source: Blacksmith Institute

UNSAFE WATER, POISONED LAND

Polluted water is unsafe for animals, plants, and humans. Oil spills are particularly disastrous. When BP's *Deepwater Horizon* rig blew up in the Gulf of Mexico in 2010, its leaking oil harmed or killed an estimated 82,000 birds, 6,000 sea turtles, 26,000 marine mammals, and a massive number of fish.

Polluted water harms the growth of plants by depleting **nutrients**, the nourishing substances in the soil. Plants may absorb contaminants from polluted water. Contaminated plants can affect the health of animals or humans who eat them.

When **solid waste** such as discarded household or industrial materials breaks down, it can pollute water and land. In Erode, India, for example, solid waste was stored in open dumps. Rainwater flowed over the waste and it became polluted. Some of the polluted rainwater seeped into the **groundwater**, the water beneath Earth's surface. This water is pumped from wells for household and industrial use. As a result, the area's well water became unsafe to drink or to use for agriculture.

Toxic waste is waste that contains dangerous substances known to cause cancer or other diseases. In the 1970s, residents of Love Canal, an area of Niagara Falls, New York, discovered toxic waste oozing into their basements, backyards, and a school. The ooze sickened children and pets, and is also believed to have caused birth defects. Hundreds of families had to leave their homes.

Explore the Issue

1. **Analyze Causes** Why are automobiles such a danger to air quality?

2. **Identify Problems and Solutions** In what ways is solid waste a threat to human health?

The Global Problem

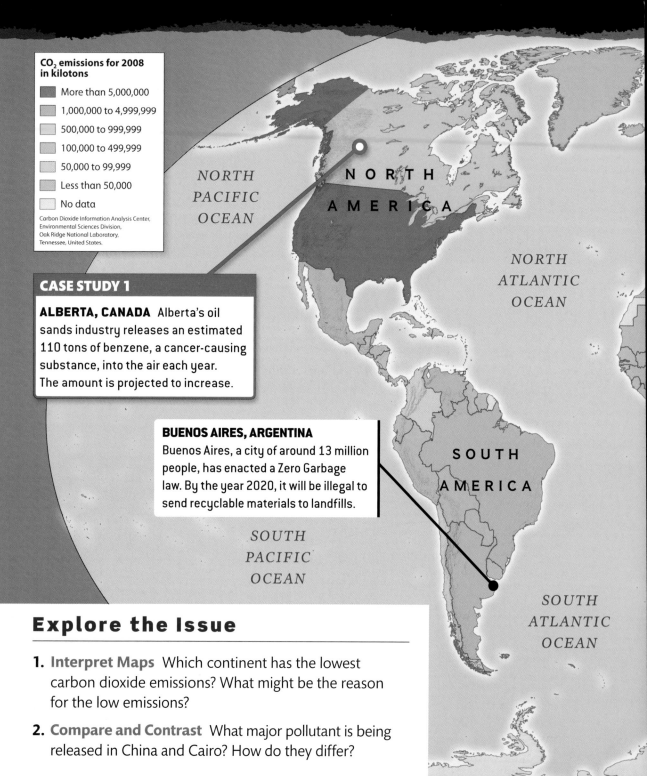

CO_2 emissions for 2008 in kilotons

- More than 5,000,000
- 1,000,000 to 4,999,999
- 500,000 to 999,999
- 100,000 to 499,999
- 50,000 to 99,999
- Less than 50,000
- No data

Carbon Dioxide Information Analysis Center, Environmental Sciences Division, Oak Ridge National Laboratory, Tennessee, United States.

NORTH PACIFIC OCEAN

NORTH AMERICA

NORTH ATLANTIC OCEAN

CASE STUDY 1

ALBERTA, CANADA Alberta's oil sands industry releases an estimated 110 tons of benzene, a cancer-causing substance, into the air each year. The amount is projected to increase.

BUENOS AIRES, ARGENTINA
Buenos Aires, a city of around 13 million people, has enacted a Zero Garbage law. By the year 2020, it will be illegal to send recyclable materials to landfills.

SOUTH AMERICA

SOUTH PACIFIC OCEAN

SOUTH ATLANTIC OCEAN

Explore the Issue

1. **Interpret Maps** Which continent has the lowest carbon dioxide emissions? What might be the reason for the low emissions?

2. **Compare and Contrast** What major pollutant is being released in China and Cairo? How do they differ?

# of Pollution

Study the map below to learn about examples of pollution across the world.

ARCTIC OCEAN

EUROPE

ASIA

AFRICA

AUSTRALIA

ANTARCTICA

INDIAN OCEAN

SOUTH-PACIFIC OCEAN

CASE STUDY 2

RUSSIA An estimated 2 billion tons of toxic waste contaminates the country of Russia. Amounts of waste range from approximately 32 tons to 800 tons within 1 square mile.

CHINA Scientists now believe that air pollution in eastern China is causing less rain to fall and that the resulting drought is reducing agricultural yields.

CAIRO, EGYPT Air pollution in Cairo is between 10 and 100 times the amount considered safe. The main pollutants include dust, soot, hydrocarbons, and lead, all of which can cause cancer.

GREAT BARRIER REEF, AUSTRALIA Pollution seriously threatens the existence of this oceanic ecosystem. Among the major contaminants are oil leaks, runoff from mining and farming, and toxic chemicals.

N
W—E
S

| 0 | 1,000 | 2,000 Miles |
| 0 | 1,000 | 2,000 Kilometers |

CANADA'S Oil Sands

Underneath this beautiful landscape in Alberta, Canada, lies one of the richest oil sands reserves on the continent.

THE WORLD'S MOST DESTRUCTIVE PROJECT?

Is the Canadian province of Alberta home to "the most destructive project on Earth?" According to Environmental Defence, a Canadian environmental organization, the answer is yes.

The project in question involves Alberta's **oil sands** deposits. Oil sands, also called *tar sands,* are a mixture of sand, clay, water, and **bitumen**. Bitumen is a heavy, thick oil. The oil sands lie beneath the floor of the forests that blanket a third of Canada and more than half of Alberta province. To reach the oil near the surface, oil companies cut down the trees. Then they remove brush and soil from the forest floor to uncover the oil sands. After the sands are processed, the companies replant trees to repair the environment. Forest restoration will take years.

SECOND LARGEST OIL RESERVES

Alberta's oil sands are estimated to contain more than 170 billion barrels of recoverable oil. This amount is second only to the oil reserves of Saudi Arabia. The oil in oil sands was once viewed as too costly to extract and process. Two things happened to push oil companies to reconsider extracting oil from oil sands as an option. The cost of oil rose to around $100 a barrel, and worldwide consumer demand for oil increased.

Some view oil sands as at least a partial answer to the world's ever-growing demand for energy. The United States, for example, imports more oil from Canada than from any other country including Saudi Arabia. The imported oil, which is roughly 50 percent oil sands, reduces U.S. dependency on Southwest Asian oil. Reducing our need for oil from Southwest Asia is viewed as a healthy economic position.

Others believe that the harmful effects of the oil sands are too great a price to pay. The extracting of oil sands poses risks to the environment and to animals and people living in the area. Moving the oil sands to processing plants in the United States means moving the material through thousands of miles of pipeline across the United States. Critics believe there are many dangers in doing so.

FROM OIL SANDS TO OIL

It takes about 2 tons of sand to produce a single barrel of oil. Oil sands that are near the surface are mined from open pits. In open-pit mining, electric shovels that are five stories high dig up oil sands deposits near the surface. Then enormous trucks haul loads weighing as much as 320 tons to an extraction plant. There, hot water and giant sifters separate the bitumen from the sand. Once it is skimmed off, the bitumen is piped to refineries in Canada and the United States. Sending bitumen through pipelines requires more pressure and heat than conventional oil. That means pipelines carrying bitumen are more likely to leak.

A handful of oil sand contains about 15 percent bitumen.

Where bitumen lies deep underground, high-pressure steam is injected through a well. The steam heats the bitumen to liquefy it. Then it is pumped to the surface and processed. This use of steam requires more energy than open-pit mining.

A giant shovel loads oil sands into a waiting truck. Some loads weigh as much as 320 tons.

ENERGY CONSUMPTION, TOXIC WASTE

Processing oil sands requires a great deal of energy. Often the energy demands exceed what it typically takes to process conventional oil. Every day a million tons of sand are mixed with more than 47 million gallons of water. The water must be heated, requiring large amounts of energy. The giant trucks that haul the sand burn 50 gallons of diesel fuel an hour.

Wastewater is dumped into huge **tailings** ponds. Tailings are the residue of the mining process. In the ponds, clay and silt settle to the bottom, where they produce a toxic sludge. The sludge poisons the pond water with chemicals.

Tailings ponds can also leak. In one Canadian incident, scientists estimated that as much as 45,000 gallons of contaminated water were reaching the Athabasca River every day. Another problem is that processing oil sands releases carbon dioxide, a greenhouse gas that most scientists believe contributes to the warming of Earth's atmosphere.

The pollution caused by the mining of oil sands threatens human health.

A biologist retrieves a sampling device from the Athabaska River. The biologist is looking for chemical contaminants from oil sand extraction plants located near the river.

ENERGY AT A PRICE

The pollution caused by the mining of oil sands threatens human health. For example, every year Alberta's mines release an estimated 110 tons of **benzene**, a cancer-causing substance, into the air. In communities downstream from the mines, unusually high numbers of people suffer from a variety of cancers and other serious health conditions.

Another form of air pollution, **acid rain**, occurs when sulfur oxides and nitrogen oxides are released into the air during the processing phase. The oxides interact with water molecules in the air to form acid rain. Acid rain speeds up the creation of a toxic form of mercury that ends up in fish, as well as in animals and humans who eat the fish.

Water pollution from oil sands mining has also affected the area's wildlife. Deformed fish and game have begun to appear. These conditions correspond to increased levels of mercury and other toxic substances in the area's sediment and water.

REDUCING POLLUTION

How can we fix the pollution problems caused by oil sands processing? Government limits on environmental pollution, as well as strict enforcement of environmental regulations, would help to reduce the pollution caused by mining oil sands.

Another possible solution is to use available technologies to reduce air pollution within refineries. An example is a carbon dioxide capture and storage project that would capture and compress the carbon dioxide into a liquid. The liquid would be piped into underground wells. Another method to reduce oil sands pollution is to convert waste into a dry form, rather than storing it in tailings ponds that leak into rivers and groundwater.

The difficult problems created by the oil sands processing will require some very creative solutions—and considerable money.

Explore the Issue

1. **Analyze Cause and Effect** Why was the mining of oil sands seen as a solution to the demand for oil?

2. **Form and Support Opinions** Do you think the oil sands industry is worth the level of pollution it produces? Explain your answer.

Children are reflected in a puddle that is probably polluted with radioactive waste. It illustrates the poor understanding of the residents about the dangers of the waste.

Russia's
RADIOACTIVE
TECHA RIVER

CONTAMINATED

Russia's Techa River is one of the most polluted places on Earth. The river, which lies east of the southern Ural Mountains, is located in the province of Chelyabinsk (CHELL-yuh-binsk). In the late 1940s, a nuclear weapons facility began dumping nuclear waste into the Techa, which became contaminated. **Nuclear waste** is **radioactive**, meaning that it gives off **radiation**—particles or rays of energy. When released into the environment, radiation is extremely dangerous to all living things.

The amount of nuclear contamination in and around the Techa River is far greater than that created by the Chernobyl nuclear disaster. In 1986, a reactor at a nuclear power plant in Chernobyl, Ukraine, exploded. It spread radioactive fallout, or particles, over tens of thousands of square miles. The Chernobyl disaster received enormous publicity, but contamination of the Techa was a closely guarded secret.

TOXIC WASTE THREATENS 100 MILLION PEOPLE

Nuclear waste is one of many forms of hazardous or toxic waste. Others include pesticides, chemicals, and elements such as lead, arsenic, and mercury. When not disposed of properly, toxic waste poisons air, water, and land. Exposure to toxic waste increases the likelihood of developing cancer or other serious diseases or conditions. Toxic waste also causes many forms of disability, which often prevent people from living normal and productive lives.

A sign warns of radioactive danger on the Techa River. The warning is largely ignored by the local population.

Nuclear waste is especially dangerous because it gives off radiation that makes people ill and that also can cause severe birth defects. Once released into the environment, radiation remains dangerous for more than 100,000 years.

A recent assessment of more than 2,000 polluted sites found health risks to more than 100 million people.

THE TECHA REGION TURNS TOXIC

The Mayak Chemical Combine was built in the 1940s to produce nuclear weapons. In the early years of its operation, Mayak dumped 2.6 billion cubic feet of radioactive waste into the Techa River. Scientists estimate that the resulting radiation equals the amount released by a small atomic bomb. When the Techa flooded in 1951, its waters spilled onto the riverbanks, contaminating the soil.

The Techa River region experienced an earlier radiation exposure in 1957. A cooling system failure caused the temperature of the radioactive waste in one of the Mayak storage tanks to rise. The tank exploded with a force equal to that of 75 tons of dynamite. Most of the radiation remained near the complex. However, some of it formed a five-mile-wide radioactive cloud that traveled across about 600 miles of Chelyabinsk province.

The accident exposed more than 250,000 people to radiation. This caused a significant increase in the number of people hospitalized during the following two years. The radiation also contaminated soil, making it dangerous to grow crops. Meat and dairy products were affected as well.

Moderately dangerous nuclear waste is often stored in concrete tanks. Sometimes the tanks are above ground and at other times the tanks are buried underground.

MORE EXPOSURE

After years of dumping into the Techa, Mayak built a facility to store nuclear waste underground in steel and concrete tanks. While Mayak was building its storage facility, the complex dumped nuclear waste into nearby Lake Karachay. Years later, that would prove to be a disastrous decision.

In 1965 and 1966, unusually dry weather caused some of the water in Lake Karachay to evaporate, which exposed radioactive sediment on the lakebed. In 1967, strong winds picked up the radioactive dry sediment and spread it over an area about the size of Maryland. The radiation affected an estimated 400,000 people.

The sign in front of an abandoned school forbids the gathering of mushrooms, the picking of berries, and fishing on the Techa River.

A researcher measures radiation levels on the banks of the Techa River. In 2010, the levels of radiation were dangerously high.

LIVING WITH TOXIC WASTE

The radiation in Chelyabinsk has taken a heavy toll on those who live in the area. Evacuation of people in the area was one way to protect them from radiation. However, there were delays before people living near the Techa were evacuated. By that time, many had been exposed to harmful doses of radiation.

Among the people who were not evacuated were those living in the town of Muslyumova (muh-sly-uh-MOH-vuh). The townspeople were not aware of the radiation and its effects, and they continued to drink the river water and use it for irrigation. They raised crops on the polluted land and allowed their animals to graze there. Plants absorbed radiation from the water and the soil. When animals and humans ate the contaminated plants, the harmful radiation affected them as well.

Today in Muslyumova, many people are suffering from illnesses caused by radiation. Rates of cancer, including leukemia and skin cancers, are two to four times as high as normal. One third of babies are born with defects or physical disorders.

CLEANING UP THE RIVER

Early efforts to clean up the Techa River had little effect. Although Mayak stopped dumping its radioactive waste, the damage had already been done. Soil and water were contaminated by radiation. Recently efforts were made to remove radioactive sludge from riverbanks in the area. The polluted soils were placed in a remote area and covered with clean soil.

The effort to clean up the Techa River and its environment is a challenging one. However, each step taken will help make the environment safer for all living things. The lessons learned will also help groups find ways to improve environments damaged by radioactive pollution.

Explore the Issue

1. **Compare and Contrast** Why is nuclear contamination more dangerous than many other forms of pollution?

2. **Draw Conclusions** Why has the cleanup of the Techa region been so challenging?

The Great Floating Garbage Patch

Plastic sample jars show material that was collected from the Great Pacific Garbage Patch.

THE GREAT FLOATING GARBAGE PATCH

The world's largest garbage dump is floating in the Pacific Ocean. It is the Great Floating Garbage Patch, with an estimated 3 million tons of garbage. Unfortunately, it's getting bigger every day. The garbage is caught up in a **gyre**, a huge circular current that occurs on the surface of the ocean.

The patch is actually two masses of trash. Floating between California and Hawaii, the Eastern Garbage Patch is estimated to be twice the size of Texas. The Western Garbage Patch is located west of Hawaii and east of Japan. The Western Patch is estimated at twice the size of France. Connecting the two is a ribbon of ocean current 6,000 miles long. The current gathers and transports the trash.

FOREVER PLASTIC

Plastic makes up 90 percent of the trash that accumulates in the ocean. In 2006, the United Nations Environment Program estimated that 46,000 pieces of plastic were floating in every square mile of ocean.

Across the globe about 3 billion plastic bottles are thrown away, along with between 500 billion and 1 trillion plastic bags every year! Once a plastic bottle or any other plastic item is made, it continues to exist. Because plastic cannot break down into harmless substances, it does not go away. Plastic products degrade over time, creating smaller and smaller pieces. These pieces are called **microplastics**. Marine life often mistake the microplastic pieces for food and swallow them. The plastic causes the animal to die.

National Geographic Emerging Explorer David de Rothschild decided to create awareness about the plastic pollution by setting out on an adventure using a boat made of plastic bottles.

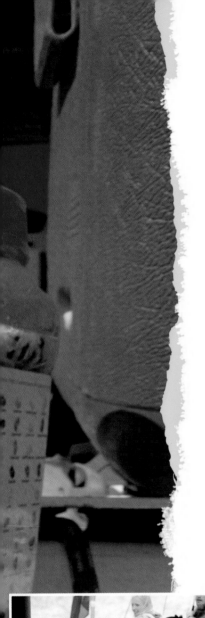

David de Rothschild is the captain of the *Plastiki*, a boat made of 12,500 recycled plastic bottles. He is shaking hands with Ian Kiernan, a leading conservationist in Australia.

> **"[The Garbage Patch] is like a soup, millions and millions of tiny fragments of plastic, suspended in the water."** —David de Rothschild

THE *PLASTIKI*

David de Rothschild believes that saving the planet can be an adventure. De Rothschild set about building the *Plastiki*, a 60-foot plastic catamaran (a boat with parallel twin hulls) that would be kept afloat by 12,500 plastic bottles.

To demonstrate **sustainability**, which is the use of natural resources without destroying the ecological balance of an area, de Rothschild added solar panels to the *Plastiki*. Bicycle-powered turbines also served as energy sources. The *Plastiki* included recycled materials and used renewable energy sources. Renewable energy sources are those resources that cannot be used up, such as sunlight, falling water, or wind.

On March 20, 2010, the explorer set sail with a small crew, including a filmmaker from National Geographic, to explore the Eastern Garbage Patch. De Rothschild and his crew spent four months at sea, eating canned and dehydrated food and taking saltwater showers during their 8,000-mile journey from San Francisco, California, to Sydney, Australia.

The *Plastiki* faced huge ocean swells, high winds, and torn sails on its 8,000-mile journey.

GARBAGE SOUP

On their journey, De Rothschild and his crew discovered the garbage patch was not just junk floating in the water. According to de Rothschild, the garbage patch is "like a soup, millions and millions of tiny fragments of plastic, suspended in the water, [most of which are] microscopic."

Charles Moore, discoverer of the garbage patch, says it is not possible to clean up the plastic. All we can do is to not make it larger. To slow the amount of plastic ending up in the oceans, de Rothschild suggests not using plastic bags for shopping.

The National Geographic film *Plastiki: 12,000 Bottle Boat* documents the story of the *Plastiki*. De Rothschild plans more adventures to increase awareness about threats to the planet.

Explore the Issue

1. **Draw Conclusions** Why is the Great Floating Garbage Patch a threat to the ocean environment?

2. **Synthesize** How did David de Rothschild's adventure demonstrate sustainability?

I DO?

Learn About
Recycling
—and become an activist

One way to fight pollution is to practice waste reduction by recycling. Becoming informed about your local recycling program is the first step to fully supporting it and will enable you to educate others about the importance of reducing waste. If your community does not have a recycling program, research a program in a neighboring municipality. Then develop and present a proposal to your local officials about the need to establish one.

IDENTIFY

- Find out whether your community has a program to recycle waste.

- Identify the area of local government that is responsible for the program.

- Determine who would be a knowledgeable person to interview about recycling as a means of managing waste in your community.

ORGANIZE

- Decide what information you want to acquire and then prepare a list of relevant questions.

- Schedule an interview and a visit to the recycling center.

- If possible, also arrange to visit a landfill to gather information about recyclables that end up there.

- Determine ways to measure the success of the community program.

Students help with a recycling project for computers and electronics.

DOCUMENT

- Ask the interviewee the questions you prepared. Collect any information available from the recycling facility.

- Inquire about and take notes on ways to increase community participation.

- Record, videotape, or take notes during your interview.

- Take photos or videotape the steps in the recycling process.

SHARE

- Use your photos and videos to create a multimedia presentation explaining the importance of recycling and how community members can participate.

- Write an article for your local paper on recycling.

- Based on what you have learned, present one or more suggestions to your school board or principal regarding how to increase recycling and reduce waste in your school.

Research & WRITE
Informative

Write an Informative Article

Polluted indoor air is becoming a health issue of increasing concern. Because people are spending an increasing amount of time indoors, everyone should have a thorough understanding of the causes, risks, and remedies associated with indoor pollution. Your assignment is to research and write about air pollution in your home and your school.

RESEARCH

Use the Internet, books, and articles to research the following questions.

- What kinds of air pollution occur indoors and how does each threaten human health?
- What causes each type of indoor air pollution?
- How can you determine the type and amount of pollution that may be contaminating the air in your home or school?
- What are some ways to reduce indoor air pollution?

As you conduct your research, take notes. Be sure to keep track of the sources you use in your research.

DRAFT

Review your notes and then write a first draft that is at least three paragraphs long.

- The first paragraph, or introduction, should engage the reader and describe the issue of air pollution as a potential threat to good health.
- The middle paragraph or paragraphs—the body of the article—should describe the different types of indoor air pollution, their causes, and how to prevent, reduce, or eliminate them.
- Be sure to use relevant facts, quotations, or other information and examples to explain indoor pollution.
- Use appropriate transitions to create cohesion, so that your information is connected to your main idea.
- You may want to include a chart, graph, or table to support your point.
- The third paragraph, or conclusion, should explain the importance of reducing indoor air pollution.

REVISE & EDIT

Look over your first draft.

- Does it provide a clear explanation of indoor air pollution and its potential threat to good health?
- Have you developed the topic with relevant facts, quotations, or other information and examples?
- Does the conclusion adequately address the importance of reducing indoor air pollution?

Review the article to make sure that you have answered all these questions. Then check your paper for spelling and punctuation errors.

PUBLISH & PRESENT

Have your teacher help you identify an appropriate environmental Web site or blog on which to publish your article. Once the information is online, inform your school and local libraries and your local newspaper of the Internet address where your article appears.

Visual GLOSSARY

pollution

toxic waste

acid rain *n.*, a form of pollution caused by the interaction of sulphur oxides, nitrogen oxides, and water

benzene *n.*, a cancer-causing substance

bitumen *n.*, thick heavy oil

carbon dioxide *n.*, a greenhouse gas

contaminant *n.*, a poisonous substance

groundwater *n.*, the water beneath Earth's surface

gyre *n.*, a circular oceanic current

microplastics *n.*, tiny particles of plastic

nuclear waste *n.*, radioactive waste

nutrient *n.*, a nourishing substance

oil sands *n.*, a mixture of sand, clay, water, and oil; also called tar sands

particulate *n.*, a tiny bit of matter

pollution *n.*, contamination of the environment

radiation *n.*, a particle or ray of energy

radioactive *adj.*, giving off radiation

solid waste *n.*, discarded household or industrial materials

sustainability *n.*, the use of renewable resources without destroying the ecological balance

tailings *n.*, mining residue

toxic waste *n.*, solid waste that contains dangerous substances

contaminant

solid waste

sustainability

INDEX

SKILLS

THE GLOBAL ISSUES SERIES

The *Global Issues* series explores relevant and compelling issues in the world today.

CLIMATE CHANGE
Many scientists have observed increasing temperatures, melting glaciers, and other possible effects of changing climate. How are countries dealing with the impact?

ENERGY RESOURCES
Providing energy to an industrialized world is a tremendous challenge. Countries around the world are experimenting with renewable energy resources.

FOOD SUPPLY
People are using their creativity and ingenuity to improve the ability to grow food for the expanding global population.

GLOBALIZATION
Free trade, migration, media, and other cultural influences are having a worldwide impact on every aspect of modern life, from food to fashion.

HABITAT PRESERVATION
The natural habitats for animals and plants are threatened around the world, but people are taking extraordinary steps to preserve those habitats before it is too late.

HEALTH
Providing quality health care and medicine is a challenge. Science and technology are finding new ways to care for people across the globe.

HUMAN RIGHTS
The United Nations passed the Declaration of Human Rights in 1948. Millions of people around the world are gaining rights like democracy, education, and economic security.

MIGRATION
Because of modern transportation and economic opportunity, people can migrate more easily from one country to another. Migration creates both challenges and opportunities for countries.

POLLUTION
Pollution of the air, water, and soil has been a problem since industrialization in the 19th century, but countries are trying some interesting new approaches to solving this problem.

POPULATION GROWTH
Explore how different countries are meeting the challenges of growing populations through education and economic opportunity.

STANDARD OF LIVING
Countries around the world are working to increase the standard of living for their populations.

WATER RESOURCES
Water is essential for life. Many countries have developed innovative ways to improve the availability and quality of water.

POLLUTION

THE
GLOBAL ISSUES
SERIES

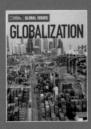
CLIMATE CHANGE

ENERGY RESOURCES

FOOD SUPPLY

GLOBALIZATION

HABITAT PRESERVATION

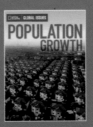
HEALTH

HUMAN RIGHTS

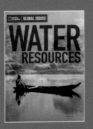
MIGRATION

POPULATION GROWTH

STANDARD OF LIVING

WATER RESOURCES

NATIONAL GEOGRAPHIC LEARNING | CENGAGE Learning

888-915-3276   NGL.Cengage.com

ISBN 978-0-7362-9785-1

90000>

9 780736 297851